anythink

Fire Trucks

Norman D. Graubart

press.

New York

Published in 2015 by The Rosen Publishing Group, Inc.
29 East 21st Street, New York, NY 10010

First Edition

Editor: Katie Kawa
Book Design: Jonathan J. D'Rozario

Photo Credits: Cover Matthew Strauss/Shutterstock.com; back cover Photoraidz/Shutterstock.com; pp. 4, 7, 8, 11, 12, 15, 16, 19, 20, 23 debra hughes/Shutterstock.com; pp. 5, 24 (fire station) steve estvanik/Shutterstock.com; pp. 6, 24 (firefighter) Jacom Stephens/E+/Getty Images; p. 9 Knumina Studios/Shutterstock.com; pp. 10, 24 (hose) Great Art Productions/Photographer's Choice/Getty Images; p. 13 KBF Media/Shutterstock.com; p. 14 Serenethos/Shutterstock.com; p. 17 Sergey Ryzhov/Shutterstock.com; pp. 18, 24 (siren) Thomas M Perkins/Shutterstock.com; p. 21 blurAZ/Shutterstock.com; p. 22 Fuse/Getty Images.

Library of Congress Cataloging-in-Publication Data

Graubart, Norman D., author.
 Fire trucks / Norman D. Graubart.
    pages cm. — (Giants on the road)
 Includes bibliographical references and index.
 ISBN 978-1-4994-0108-0 (pbk.)
 ISBN 978-1-4994-0111-0 (6 pack)
 ISBN 978-1-4994-0105-9 (library binding)
 1. Fire engines—Juvenile literature. I. Title.
 TH9372.G73 2015
 628.9'259—dc23
                                    2014025287

Manufactured in the United States of America

CPSIA Compliance Information: Batch #CW15PK: For Further Information contact Rosen Publishing, New York, New York at 1-800-237-9932

Contents

Fire trucks are kept at places called **fire stations**.

Fire trucks bring **firefighters** to places that are on fire.

The firefighter who drives the truck is called the engineer.

Fire trucks carry long **hoses**. The hoses are used to put water on fires.

Fire trucks also have ladders.

13

Ladders are on the top of fire trucks.

Ladders help firefighters
reach people in tall buildings.

Fire trucks are really loud!
The **siren** tells everyone
a fire truck is on the road.

Fire trucks are allowed
to go faster than regular cars
when they're driving to a fire.

You can visit the fire station in your town to see fire trucks!

Words to Know

firefighter

fire station

hose

siren

Index

F
firefighters, 7, 8, 16
fire stations, 4, 23

H
hoses, 11

L
ladders, 12, 15, 16

Websites

Due to the changing nature of Internet links, PowerKids Press has developed an online list of websites related to the subject of this book. This site is updated regularly. Please use this link to access the list: www.powerkidslinks.com/gotr/ftr